Into the Garden of Dreams

Pathways to Imagination for 5 – 8s

A relaxing resource for teachers
to help raise children's self-esteem
and expression in the classroom

With photocopiable ideas for easy reference

Preface

This teaching resource originated in a self-esteem package that I designed for in-service training, with teachers in various schools including my own.

All the activities have been practised very successfully with early years and primary children. My Primary 2 class would often ask specifically for a number of the activities and as a department we use them regularly. We have all found that using daily exercises and breathing brings a calmness and alertness into the classroom.

My personal feeling is that the visualizations are the strongest and most creative part of the material. They enable children to deal with personal development issues in a safe environment.

I want to express my gratitude to both my Head and Depute Head Teachers for encouraging me to develop this material, and to use it with the children. I also appreciate the enthusiasm with which colleagues have applied the ideas in their own classrooms.

Best of all has been the response of the children. Thanks indeed to them.

Linda-Jane Simpson

Published by Brilliant Publications, 1 Church View, Sparrow Hall Farm, Edlesborough, Dunstable LU6 2ES

Written by Linda-Jane Simpson
Edited by Marie Birkinshaw
Designed by Anne Matthews
Ilustrated by Andrew Everitt-Stewart
Additional illustrations contributed
  by children at the author's school

© Linda-Jane Simpson 2001
ISBN 1 897675 76 3
First published in 2001
Reprinted 2003
10 9 8 7 6 5 4 3 2

Introduction

The aim of this book is to offer a range of enjoyable activities and games to help raise self-esteem and expression in the classroom. Through relaxation techniques and visualizations, pathways are followed into the 'Garden of Dreams' – a gateway into the imagination of children, aged 5-8.

The book is divided into two parts:

The Teacher's handbook should be read first. It explains the value of self-esteem in the curriculum and provides helpful explanation and background to each of the activities. The handbook suggests three tested routes:

Route 1   Self-esteem activities and games

Route 2   Visualizations to explore the 'Garden of Dreams'

Route 3   Creative ideas for expressive work

Each route links directly into the practical step-by-step suggestions, or Pathways, that are provided separately as photocopiable sheets for ease of reference.

The **photocopiable sheets** give detailed instructions for each of the 32 Pathways. These can be photocopied for easy use in the classroom or as an in-school teacher training resource. The *supplementary resources* at the end of this section are blank photocopy masters for the children's work.

The Route 2 visualizations, which introduce meditative moments to the school day, are best used in the sequence in which they appear. The basic journey must be used first, since it introduces the children not only to features of the garden, but also to basic meditative behaviour, stillness and silence with closed eyes.

Contents

Contents

The importance of self-esteem

First, some useful reminders:

- Self-concept has a powerful influence on a child's learning.

- Children's beliefs and attitudes about themselves are learned and can be changed over a period of time.

- Teachers can foster in children a 'can do' attitude across a wide range of activities.

- Children can also gain a sense of success from each other – peer support and approval.

- Children will take risks and function well on every level if, within their classroom environment, they are valued and there is trust, support, care and openness.

- The teacher can greatly facilitate self-esteem by having high, positive yet realistic expectations, and by encouraging investigation and inquiry.

- The children will need opportunities for thought, choice, responsibility and dialogue.

- Self-esteem will be raised if the teacher listens to the children, allows them time for reflection and gives genuine, focused praise.

- Building up self-esteem will help you make your children *'Winners'*.

Winners

To make your class into *Winners* say to them –

Self-esteem through the curriculum

Two expressive areas of the curriculum can greatly enhance the development of positive self-esteem.

Art reflects children's growing awareness of people, both of themselves and of others. Through creative work children develop skills, imagination, self-discipline and the capacity to make decisions and solve problems.

Through drawing, particularly, children extend their social self out into the world of reality and communicate their responses to experiences.

The effects of this expression are two-fold. The children get some idea of their own value from any feedback such interaction brings. Art activities also provide the teacher with a window into the thoughts and feelings of any child and help to indicate levels of their self-esteem.

Drama extends the children's own capacity for imaginative play, by involving the class and teacher in role-play within the drama story. The story becomes real for that instant, and real enough to involve the children at a deeper level. From the safety of knowing that it is all make-believe, the children can explore feelings and relationships, and ways of dealing with situations and problems.

Since drama uses what pupils bring to it from their own experience, it highlights where they are in their thinking, and helps to extend them beyond what they already know.

The children's self confidence develops from this knowledge of life, gained through dramatic play, and from having to speak and express themselves in any role they assume.

Putting the SELF into self-esteem

Self regard   positive self regard means all children can achieve their best

Encourage   encourage children to like themselves, use praise, rewards, celebration

Learner   be a learner too; solve all kinds of problems together

Facial expression   use facial expression, as well as eye contact, tone of voice, stance and gesture; children read these signals too

Eye contact   eye contact while you actively listen to children

Stimulate   stimulate their imaginations

Think   train the children to think in images, 'what you think is what you are'

Each child   reach each child, seek everyone's contribution

Ever genuine   be ever genuine, sincere and realistic in your praise

Messages   messages must be clear; vary the methods to suit the needs of the listeners

Teacher's handbook

Route 1: Self-esteem activities and games

Coordination and breathing exercises

1: Finger exercises

2: Hand exercises

3: Arm exercises

4: Arm and leg exercises

5: Breathing exercises

6: Full moons

7: Palm trees

Pathways 1 – 7 were designed to develop confidence and self-awareness by using breathing and exercise techniques. They also increase dexterity, coordination and calm, making everyone feel lighter and more energetic.

It is well worth spending 10 – 20 minutes daily enhancing the children's self-esteem using the activities, following the instructions given. They can be done with or without music.

The table on page 11 summarizes some of these exercises. Vary the exercises by choosing something from each box each day. The teacher will need to model each exercise for the children, until they become familiar with it.

The table can be enlarged for display in the classroom to encourage the children to do the exercises themselves in odd moments.

Teacher's handbook

Fingers	Hands
Shaker	Scrunch
Robins pecking crumbs	Piano player
Prayer rockets	Twin lift
Interlacers	I hear spiders
Open and close	
Church and steeple	
Palm rub	
Down in the valleys	
Arms	**Arms and legs**
This way and that way	Knee circles
Rope pull	Hip circles
Circle stretch	Cross over
Swimmer	Diagonal jumps
Soldiers	Tap behind your back

Teacher's handbook

Self-esteem games

Pathways 8–12 provide powerful ideas for relaxing group games that will help to focus the children and which are particularly useful at the beginning of a lesson.

The sharing ring offers an opportunity to talk and share ideas on any subject, e.g. within a drama lesson, after a visualization, for a brainstorming session, or when there is an important issue to deal with. Encourage the children to share their feelings if they want to, following the teacher's role model.

Teacher's handbook

Building a sense of individual self-worth

Pathways 13 – 19 offer practical activities that will build up an appreciation of self-worth for each individual child.

Each child gets to be a star person for a day, and on another occasion can share an object of their choice with the rest of the class. They are awarded a birthday or star badge (Supplementary resources A/B).

The Tin Men sheets (Supplementary resources C/D) can be used as a stimulus for the children to talk about, and record, their perceived abilities, talents, preferences and personal qualities. They each have a different focus; the first sheet is for recording their responses to school subjects, while the second centres on personal qualities and social skills.

With the help of the teacher, the child completes the face in each section of the patchwork according to what they feel. They then go back over the Tin Man, putting in their own symbol for 'I am good at' in the sections they feel are appropriate.

The value of object-sharing

Pathway 17 requires the teacher to role model the activity. The interesting object chosen is kept a strict secret once placed in the surprise box.

This activity can be done once a day, each day, or once a week at a certain time. The children are usually eager for their turn. They can be praised for particularly interesting objects and for answering well. It develops both questioning and answering skills. It highlights for the children which questions are most effective in getting to the information, and how information can be pieced together. It also becomes clear to the children that answers need to be thought out, so as not to give too much information away too soon.

A photocopy master of an explanatory letter to parents is available in Supplementary resources F. A sheet put inside the surprise box, may help the children prepare their answers at home. It could contain the following information.

SURPRISE BOX

1 Choose your surprise object
2 Put it inside this box
3 Take it back to school
4 Keep it a secret
5 Let the class ask clue questions
6 Be ready to answer these questions

How does it sound in the box?
Is it hard or soft?
What letter does it begin with?
Is it rough or smooth?
Do you play with it?
Where did you find it in your house?

What is it made of?
What do you use it for?
Does it do a job?
Can you eat with it?
What is the last letter of the word?

7 Answer the questions carefully

Route 2: Visualizations to explore the Garden of Dreams

Background

Route 2 uses the comfort and safety of a welcoming garden, the features of which become very familiar the more the children visit the garden.

The things to see there are simple and few in number. They also relate in colour to a rainbow and to the chakras of the body. These are the seven energy centres of the body as identified in ancient yoga teachings.

The meditative visualizations fulfil two important human functions. Firstly, they encourage the children to use the right side of their brains, as both art and drama do. It is in the right part of the brain that the imagination and the ability to 'see' pictures resides.

Secondly, these techniques also gently develop an awareness in the children of the benefits of a relaxed calm state, where for a time all is still, the mind's chatter can stop, and worries disappear.

Exercising the right side of the brain to compensate for subjects that over-use its left side, and the maintenance of a state of relaxed alertness, are all important life skills which visualization develops. The younger the children can experience their effects, the better.

Some children are more willing to go into a meditative state than others. The things which they draw, talk and write about afterwards reveal how the experience has enabled these children to reach deeper parts of their minds and emotions.

Teacher's handbook

Creating the atmosphere
Choose a reasonably quiet area or room where you are unlikely to be disturbed. There should be enough space for the children to sit or lie down, without being too close to their neighbours.

The teacher encourages and role models a *state of stillness*. Breathing, relaxation, palm trees and palming are ways of achieving this.

Visualization requires physical stillness but also *concentration and alertness of mind*. Gentle practice is the only way to develop this. The younger the children start the better. The span of concentration can be gradually extended.

The visualizations have been designed around the *image of a garden*, an inner garden. The features of the garden are revealed to them in sequence. Each time a new feature is added and it connects with the purpose of the visualization. The children quickly become familiar with the routine because the image of the garden is built up in this very progressive way. As their skills and concentration develop, each visualization takes them deeper into the garden and reveals some of its hidden treasures.

It is very important that the *teacher lowers their voice* and speaks in a slow relaxed manner. The visualization should be told in a calm, unhurried way. Pause between sentences to allow the scene to sink in, and for the children to experience it fully.

The children with short attention spans will be those who fidget. Encourage them towards ever increasing spans of stillness and insist that they are quiet to allow others to concentrate. *Praising* those who keep their eyes closed and concentrate will exert its own peer influence, as will the richer pictures which the other children will have to share.

About the Pathways

Each journey into the garden of dreams is detailed in Pathways 20–26. The journeys include:

20:	The basic journey	24:	The waterfall
21:	The worry basket	25:	Meeting Owl
22:	The healing fairies	26:	Owl's quest
23:	The golden fish		

The *basic journey* is used to begin and end all the visualizations. It gives a sense of security as it becomes familiar to the children.

The *worry basket* can be used at any time to help teachers or parents share in any issues that are concerning to a child. It could be used specifically with a very unhappy child who resists talking about a problem.

The *healing fairies* is very relaxing and healing generally, but again it is particularly effective with children who are ill or finding it difficult to get to sleep.

The golden fish attempts to get children to recognize their talents, skills and achievements and could be followed up with the Tin Man activity. The visualization tries to encourage them to give themselves praise.

The *waterfall* is a visually colourful, refreshing and cleansing experience.

Owl and *Owl's quest* are designed to get the children to visually show us how they see and represent aspects of their own unique individuality. Owl is a friendly character, in whom it would be safe to confide.

Preparation

Before beginning the visualization journey, explain the following to the children.

I am going to take you all on a journey with me.

It is a very special journey and you will all be very safe. It is a journey that will happen in our heads, in our imagination. The things you see, say, and do on this journey will happen there inside your mind. So you won't actually move or speak.

Try, if you can, to 'see' in your head the places I take you to and what we do. Close your eyes to help you see more clearly. Let your body rest, relax and be still. Have your eyes closed for the whole journey. I am going to take you to a lovely garden, that is your very own. You will find that it is very peaceful there, and nothing can harm you.

The worry basket visualization

After this particular visualization, use the Sharing ring (Pathway 10) as a means to get the children talking about what they saw or did, if they would like to do so.

Later, in private, the teacher can examine the worry slips and, because they are named, they can provide important insights into a child's feelings and current situation at school and at home.

Some happy, secure and well-balanced children may come to the teacher and say *'I have nothing to worry about'*. The teacher can reply to these children, *'That's wonderful. Write on your slip – Thank you, but I have no worries today.'*

Other children who have no real concerns may trump up issues, so as to have something to write!

What is most surprising and helpful, is how deeply a follow-up to this visualization reaches the children with real problems. It enables them to share a little of these because the information remains private, as far as they are concerned. The teacher must respect the confidentiality of any information the child discloses. It is an area that requires sensitive handling.

Teacher's handbook

Route 3: Creative ideas for expressive work

Ways to link back to the visualizations

If any creative work, such as writing or art, is done after visualization it will be noticeably richer in images. It is for this reason that I have included some follow up work to nurture this increased creativity, see Pathways 27–32. They offer ideas that link directly back into the visualizations.

27:    Drawing

28:    Painting and craft

29:    Map making

30:    Dream flags

31:    Modelling trees

32:    Activities linked specifically to Owl's Quest

Into the Garden of Dreams

Pathway 1: Finger exercises

Shaker

Shake your fingers in the air vigorously.

Robins pecking crumbs

Tap each finger in turn on the top part of your thumbs.

Prayer rockets

Place palms together and push your hands straight up above your head. Stretch up as far as you can. Lower your hands in the same way until they start to split apart. Resist this pressure, keeping them together for as long as possible, as you lower.

Interlacers

Interlace your fingers and use your palms to tap your chest three times. Then turn your hands 'outside in' and gently push them away from your body until your arms are almost straight. Move in time with the chant 'Tap your chest and push away'.

Open and close

Clench and stretch your fingers alternately. Close your fingers and make your hands as small and tight as possible. Open and stretch your fingers out into a starfish shape.

Church and steeple

Bend your fingers at the second knuckle. Place your hands together to form the church. Tap the sides of the thumbs together three times. Bring out the first fingers and then tap three times. Bring out each pair of fingers in turn and tap them. Once the pinkies have tapped, the church and steeple are complete.

Palm rub

Rub your palms briskly together. Also rub your wrists together.

Down in the valleys

Spread the fingers of your left hand wide. Tap the bottom edge of your right hand down in each of the 'valleys' between the fingers of the left hand. Change hands and repeat.

Into the Garden of Dreams

Pathway 2: Hand exercises

Scrunch

Scrunch up an A4 or A5 piece of scrap paper into a ball and squeeze. Do this with each hand in turn.

Piano player

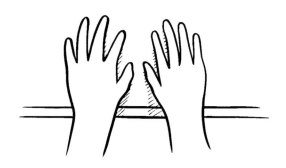

Play fast music on an imaginary piano with the fingers of both your hands. Keep both wrists on the table, so that your individual fingers are doing the work, moving up and down.

Twin lift

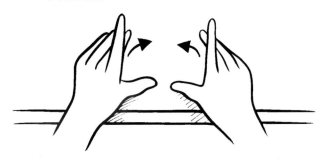

Keeping your hands flat, lift just your thumbs, then each pair of fingers in turn, and rap them on the table. An alternative is to give the fingers numbers or names, and use them to tell the children which fingers to lift and rap.

I hear spiders

Drum your fingers up and down on the table or floor. They must stop and freeze quickly, whenever I (the teacher) says 'I think I hear spiders'.

Into the Garden of Dreams

Pathway 3: Arm exercises

This way and that way

Stretch your arms out to the sides, level with your shoulders. Turn your palms first up to the sky and then down to the ground. Repeat. Arms could be moved in time with the chant 'This way and that way'.

Rope pull

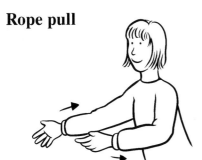

Stretch out your hands and use each hand alternately to pull on an imaginary thick rope.

Circle stretch

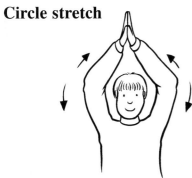

Palms together in front of your legs. Now raise your hands together above your head with arms stretched. Look up at them. Turn your palms out and separate your hands, circling them down to either side. Feel a stretch in each arm and then bring them back to their starting position. Try to 'draw' a large round shape with your hands. Repeat.

Swimmer

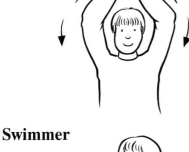

Push your hands and arms forward and then pull them back in the breast stroke.

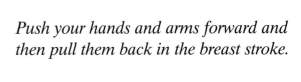

Soldiers

(1) March in time on the spot, letting your arms dangle.

(2) Swing your arms in time, as you march forwards, knees coming up.

Into the Garden of Dreams

Pathway 4: Arm and leg exercises

Knee circles

Bend your knees slightly and place one hand on each knee. Using your hands, make your knees 'draw' circles, first one way round, and then the other. Build up to twelve clockwise, and twelve anti-clockwise.

Hip circles

With your knees slightly bent, place your hands on your hips. Make circle movements gently with your hips, moving them first clockwise, then anti-clockwise. Start with six in each direction and build up to twelve rotations.

Cross over

Use your elbow to touch the opposite raised knee. Swap over and use the other elbow and knee. Repeat.

Diagonal jumps

Reach out to the side with one hand and point out the opposite foot as you jump. Repeat with the other hand and foot.

Tap behind your back

Bring one foot up behind you, by bending at the knee. Tap its heel with your opposite hand. Repeat using the other hand and foot.

Into the Garden of Dreams

Pathway 5: Breathing exercises

Breathing through your nose and mouth

Practise deliberate breathing through your nose and out through your mouth, like this…

Now 'soften' your breathing until you can hardly hear it at all. Keep your eyes closed as you pay attention to your breathing changes.

Blow-outs

Now stand up. Take a deep breath in through your nose.

Hold it and then blow it out noisily through your mouth as you flop over from the waist.

Allow your arms and head to hang. Then slowly come up, breathing in as you do so.

Do three blow-outs in a row and then hold the bent over position for a few minutes.

Blow out any unwanted emotions along with their outbreath, for example, anger or noisiness.

Shrugs

Breathe in through your nose and shrug your shoulders up towards your ears. Hold for a few seconds.

Breathe out through your mouth as you release your shoulders and let them flop downwards. Repeat.

Gradually quieten your breath and decrease the amount of shoulder movement accordingly.

Out-breath

Put your arms and hands straight out in front of you, at waist height, with your palms facing down.

As you breathe in slowly raise your hands in that position, up to neck height.

Breathe out, through your mouth, by blowing the breath out slowly, and lowering your hands slowly to the starting position.

Emphasize a slow controlled out-breath.

Into the Garden of Dreams

Pathway 6: Full moons

Stand with your feet slightly apart. Put your palms together in front of your legs, with your fingers pointing down.

Keep your hands together, and raise them high above your head, so that your arms are stretched. Look up at your hands.

Turn your palms to face outwards and separate your hands, circling them down to either side, and back to their starting position.

Imagine you are drawing a large full moon shape with your hands. Repeat.

Breathe in as you raise your hands. Hold your breath, with your hands stretched above your head. Breathe out slowly as you lower your hands down to your sides.

(for children familiar with the movement ask them to repeat the following while they move their arms and hands)

- *'Anything I do will need me to focus'* (palms together in front)

- *'It can help if I reach up into my imagination'* (hands stretched up above your head)

- *'I can reach out beyond myself to talk and listen with others'* (hands straight out to the sides)

- *'I know that I can always come back to me'* (palms together again).

Repeat the circle movement again, and say the following together:

- *'Life is about being involved'* (reach up)

- *'It needs me to offer my own ideas'* (reach out to the sides)

- *'It is about taking on different roles'* (bring hands down)

- *'I will always be safe'* (palms together).

Into the Garden of Dreams

Pathway 7: Palm trees

Get the children to stand still in a space with their feet together, their hands resting on their hips, and their eyes closed.

Then take the children on a mini visualization in which they pretend to be palm trees.

Imagine your feet are the roots of a tall palm tree sunk down into the sand of a clear quiet beach.

Your legs and body are the trunk of the tree and your arms are the branches. These palm trees are growing at the edge of a beach on a beautiful island. There is clear blue sea all around.

A breeze blows round the island and it ruffles the palms, gently moving them to and fro. It is very peaceful. There is only the sound of the breeze and of the tide. The waves are coming up onto the beach… and going out… coming in… and going out.

Use 'nose and mouth' breathing (Pathway 5) to accompany this visualization. As the breathing softens, so can the arm movement. The arms should move slowly and gently, until they are hardly moving at all.

The in-breath can represent the waves coming in, and the out-breath the waves going back.

Into the Garden of Dreams

Pathway 8: Huggy bears

Version 1

In this activity the children dance in a space to music, or while the teacher sings a favourite song.

When the music stops, or the teacher stops singing, the children must all say 'Huggy bears!' and reach for whoever is nearest to them and give them a hug.

Then the dance or song continues. Emphasize to the children that they must try to hug as many different people as possible.

Version 2

This activity is basically the same as Version 1 except it has an introduction. The teacher explains that the hug is to be a silent message to each of your Huggy bear partners. Discuss what the message could be, for example, 'I think you are special' or 'I like you a lot'. The class decide together what the silent message will be and chant it in a whisper a few times before the dance begins and continues as Version 1.

Into the Garden of Dreams

Pathway 9: Squeeze games

This game works to focus the children and is useful at the beginning of a lesson.

Version 1

Stand in a large circle holding hands. The idea of the game is to pass an 'electric' message all the way round the circle by each person gently squeezing the next person's hand.

To begin with the teacher can start it off by squeezing the hand of the child next to them. The child receiving a squeeze with one hand passes it on to the next person by squeezing with their other hand.

The teacher can send the squeeze round in one direction, and then the other. The children can watch the squeeze going round, and see if one way is quicker than the other.

Once the children can pass the 'message' round quickly in either direction, the class can try the game with their hands held behind their backs.

A child could also be chosen to start the squeeze off.

Version 2

This activity is basically the same as Version 1, but has the following introduction.

The squeeze is to be a silent message of support, praise or encouragement to everyone in the circle. Ask for suggestions for what the message could be. Decide on the message and chant it in a whisper a few times before starting the squeeze.

Emphasize that each child must look at the next person as they pass on the squeeze. It is important that there is eye contact in this version.

Pathway 10: Sharing ring

The class or group are seated in a large circle, with the teacher and any other adults as part of the circle.

It is an opportunity to talk and share ideas on any subject, for example:

- Within a drama lesson

- After a visualization

- For a brainstorming session

- When there is an important issue to deal with.

Begin yourself, as a role model, then encourage the children to share their feelings if they want to.

The teacher first shares her thoughts with the children. On finishing she 'passes on the touch' to the child beside her. This is done by touching them lightly on their arm.

This child then decides whether they want to contribute at that moment. If they do not, they pass on the touch to the next child.

The information being shared is personal and there is no pressure or repercussions if a child chooses to be silent and just listen.

Very often, after the touch has gone all the way round, and everyone understands what is being asked of them, the children who opted out first time, will ask for the opportunity to speak.

Depending on the subject of the sharing ring, a lighted candle can enhance the stillness and thoughtful involvement.

Pathway 11: Relaxation

Seated

Children can sit cross legged in a space with their eyes closed or at tables, arms folded with heads resting on arms, kneeling, or with bottoms on heels.

Bring your head slowly forwards and then down till your forehead touches the table (or floor). Close your eyes.

Lying

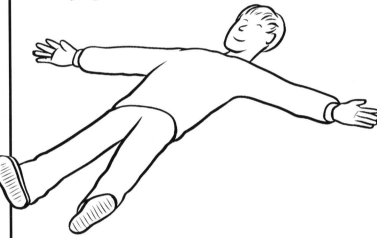

Lie flat on your back in a space.

Have your arms out at your sides with your palms up.

Put your legs straight out, with your feet falling outwards.

Close your eyes and keep as still as you can.

Palming

This is very soothing for the eyes and calming generally. It can be done quickly anywhere. *In a seated position, rub your palms together until they are warm. Place the heels of your hands gently against your eye sockets, and keep them there for a few minutes.*

Relax your body and breathe slowly. Count 1, 2, 3, then remove your hands and open your eyes slowly.

Into the Garden of Dreams

Pathway 12: Caring hands

The children choose partners and sit in a space in their twos.

One child sits in front cross-legged with their eyes closed, waiting to be relaxed.

The other child kneels up behind them using their hands to make the following stroking movements on their partner's head, shoulders, arms and back.

The movements are always done in the following order:

Snowflakes

A light pitter pattering movement with the fingertips on the head, back and arms.

Waves

Smooth sweeping flowing movements down arms and back.

Calm

Both hands are spread out and remain completely still.

The child being relaxed, points to where on their head, shoulders or back they want the calm.

The child doing the stroking can close their eyes now too, and they can try to breathe together, in harmony.

After a count of 1, 2, 3, both children slowly open their eyes.

The child being relaxed can thank their partner and comment on which of the movements they liked best.

The children then swap positions and roles.

Into the Garden of Dreams

Pathway 13: Star person

Song

The other children sing:

'Twinkle twinkle little star,
We know just who you are'.

Then they all say the child's name and the star child comes forward.

Birthday

The child can be asked about their presents and cards. Then everyone sings, 'Happy Birthday'.

Star badges

The star person can choose which friend will award them with a star birthday badge.

Special day

Make it a special day by lighting a candle or candles (one for each year) granting the child a special request.

They might ask, for example: to go out first at playtime, to play a game and they get first go for someone to sing them a song or tell them a joke, or for someone to lend them something for the day.

Into the Garden of Dreams

Pathway 14: Class applause

Class applause

The children in the class can be encouraged to applaud a class member, whenever someone has:

- Demonstrated something correctly
- Given a sensible answer
- Had a good guess
- Answered a difficult question
- Shown a change in behaviour
- Done something for someone else

You will soon find that the children applaud spontaneously when such a situation arises.

Words

Applause says, 'Well done!' to the child, and words can enhance this praise.

The teacher could role model this, adding words of encouragement or praise, and patting the child on the back.

With older children, a 'special friend' may be allowed to do this for the child, provided it is done in a sincere manner.

Song

Singing, 'For you're a jolly good fellow…' can similarly encourage self-pride in achievements of many kinds.

Standing ovation

A child could receive a standing ovation from their class and teacher, if he or she has done something to be particularly proud of.

Into the Garden of Dreams

Pathway 15: Name games

Run across the circle

The class stands in a large circle, and someone is chosen to begin.

The child starts by looking across the circle and saying the name of someone opposite them. They then run across the circle to them and sit down in their place. That person must look across and shout another person's name and run towards them.

If the children sit down after they have had a turn, it is clear to the others who is still in the game. The final person must try to remember who started the game and run to them to complete the game.

Once the children have tried out the game and understand the rules, they can be encouraged to see how quickly everyone can have a turn.

The Hello name game

In this activity a cushion or beanbag will be needed for throwing across the circle to someone.

The children stand in a large circle. First, encourage the children to think of their own greetings. These are simple but positive statements, for example, 'Hello David', 'Good morning Sally'.

Then one child is given the cushion or beanbag. They start by shouting out a greeting to another child and establishing good eye contact with them before throwing the beanbag.

If there is someone whose name they do not know, they must ask the child for it, and then throw the beanbag to that person.

Get the children to sit down once they have thrown the beanbag. The game can be played against the clock, but the beanbag must be thrown *across* the circle and not passed to a neighbour.

Into the Garden of Dreams

Brainstorm ways of making and keeping friends

Think about the kinds of things that the children could do for others that would be sincere and appreciated:

- Share things with them
- Care about them
- Play with them
- Talk with them
- Look after them
- Do things to help them
- Give them things
- Tell them jokes
- Read together
- Wave to them
- Sit together

Emphasize that these are not ways to 'buy' a friend. You put yourself out for another person. This is the essence of friendship.

Then list some things that you do not do to friends:

- Ignore them
- Leave them on their own
- Hit them
- Take their toys or sweets

Relate these lists to the school's (or class), good behaviour policy (example in Supplementary resource E).

Into the Garden of Dreams

Pathway 17: Surprise box

Find a cardboard box. A shoe box is ideal for size and firmness. Cover it with gift wrapping paper, for example, gold or holographic paper. Put it into a bag for going to and from school.

Explain the Surprise box activity to the children. Get them each to take home a copy of the letter (SR/F) that explains what the child is to do when it is their turn to bring the Surprise box.

At home the child chooses an object (not valuable) which is of interest and which no one else has brought before. They must also be able to answer questions about their object. Their chosen object is put into the Surprise Box and brought to school the next day.

In the initial stages of learning this activity, the teacher may check the contents of the box, in order to guide the child with their answers.

The Surprise box session always starts with the question, '*What does it sound like?*' The child with the box then comes up and stands in front of the others to shake the box.

Then the other children ask questions. It is important that they listen to each other's questions, so that the same questions are not repeated. The teacher must emphasize, and role play, the use of clue questions (for example, *What colour is it? What is it made of?*) rather than guess questions (*Is it a clock?*).

It is vital that the children use the answers to ask further clue questions to obtain even more information. Once enough clue questions have been asked to enable someone can make a 'good guess' then a child can try to name the object.

The child who says it correctly is the one who takes the box home next.

If the person who guessed correctly has already had a turn, then they choose someone who has not yet had the Surprise box at home.

A rota of names that are ticked off will help to keep a check of who has had a turn. In this way, the children also gain experience in using a checklist and come to understand the importance of this recording device.

Pathway 18: Why I like myself

Ask the children to name the different people they like.

If they do not say themselves, ask them: *What about yourself? Do you like you?*

Emphasize that it is very important that they like themselves.

Ask them to think about this by asking themselves these questions.

What do you like about:

- The way you look?
- How you play?
- How you act with others?
- What you do?

Talk about each category and ask the children to write their own lists.

Make a '*Why I Like Myself*' booklet using these ideas. Draw pictures and write, to show what they like about themselves.

In a sharing ring, get the children to share their books and talk about them to the class or group.

Use the two Tin Men sheets (Supplementary resources C/D) as a stimulus for the children to talk about, and record, their perceived abilities, talents, preferences and personal qualities.

Into the Garden of Dreams

Pathway 19: My self-portrait

Encourage the children to make a sketch, drawing or painting of themselves, using chalk, pencil, felt tip, ink, charcoal, crayon, pastel or paint.

These can be made from memory or by using mirrors.

It may be appropriate for the portraits to be shared with others and discussed.

Create occasions for displaying the self portraits. Birthdays and special projects provide opportunities to use the portraits.

They could be used as part of the activities connected with 'Why I Like Myself'.

Into the Garden of Dreams

Pathway 20: The basic journey

This is the basic journey on which the teacher takes the children. Further features are added on to this main section. The end section always remains the same. Start first with the preparation text from page 18 of the Teacher's handbook.

There is a garden, a beautiful garden… You will know when you are getting near to it because you will hear birds singing… Then we come to a little red gate. It has a carved sign which says 'Garden of Dreams. Everyone welcome.' It is a wooden gate that has been painted bright red. I will open it and we will all go through into the garden… Once we are in, I'll close the gate. Our feet follow a path of little orange stones. It is a winding path and it takes us past some bright yellow sunflowers. Let's stop and look at their yellow petals and big round centres… On their long stalks, they bob about in the breeze, as if they are waving.

As we move on a little, the path has green grass growing on both sides. Bend down and rub your hands through it and look at its greenness…

The path takes us up a little hill past a big old oak tree… You stretch your arms part of the way round its big trunk, and touch its rough bark… Round the back of the tree trunk, there is a little wooden ladder propped up against it… When you climb up the ladder, and look closely in amongst the leaves, you can just see a small wooden tree house…

I'll leave you there for a minute to look at the tree yourself… Look at its branches… its leaves… the little ladder and the tree house…

End Section

It is time now to leave the tree. Although we must go now, we can go back to the garden whenever we want… Let's follow the path back down the little hill… past the grass… and the yellow sunflowers… Keep following the path back to the little wooden gate.

I'll open the gate so that we can all pass by… After we have all come out, I close the gate…

I am now going to count slowly. When I have said three, open your eyes, very slowly… One… two… three… Back to the classroom. If you have been lying down, gently roll over on to one side. Now have a big stretch… Slowly… very slowly come up into a sitting position.

Into the Garden of Dreams

Pathway 21: The worry basket

Use the basic journey visualization (Pathway 20) to get the children to the big tree. Use the following to continue:

Today hanging from one of the tree's strongest branches is a large round basket with a lid. There is a label inside which says:

> *The Worry Basket. Leave any problems, worries, or*
> *fears you have in here. Don't carry them around.*

Think carefully and see if you have a worry or a problem... When you have found it... I want you to take it into your hands and scrunch it up... squeeze it up tight and small... Lift the lid of the basket and put your scrunched up worry inside... You can just drop it in, or throw it into the basket, see how you feel... There is no use you carrying your worries around.

*(Now use the **End Section** to finish.)*

Once the children are back in the present and seated in the Sharing ring, the teacher can explain the following.

'Now, we can use that worry basket, because here it is.'

The teacher can walk round the inside of the circle letting the children read the label inside.

> Worry basket. Leave any problems, worries or fears
> you have in here. Don't carry them around.

'The basket is going to stay here open in the centre of the circle and in a moment you will all go somewhere in the room by yourself to think. Then write your name and a little worry, fear or problem on a slip of paper like this.

This is just for you. No one else is to know or see what you have written. It is just for you to know.

When you have finished, fold your paper over and come back and sit in your place in the sharing circle.'

Once all the children have returned to their places, the teacher can go round and tap certain children round the circle. On this signal, they can each go forward, scrunch their worry paper up tight and put it in the basket. The teacher can role model the strong gesture and pleasure at getting rid of it. After all the worries are inside the basket, the children can chant with the teacher *'Goodbye worries!'* and the lid is firmly placed on top. The basket can be put somewhere out of sight.

Into the Garden of Dreams

Pathway 22: The healing fairies

Use the basic journey visualization (Pathway 20) to bring the children to the little ladder at the back of the big old tree. Continue as follows:

Today as you look at the ladder, you think there are little lights on each of the steps… When you take a closer look you see that each little light is actually a little fairy… They are laughing and pretending to hide from you, behind bits of the ladder… One by one they all come out, until all seven fairies are waving, and fluttering their wings in front of you… They are all smiling. Each one is a different colour of the rainbow, and carries a little duster of the same colour in their hand… red… orange… yellow… green… blue… purple… and white. They take your hands and help you climb the little ladder up to the tree house… When you get there… they all push the door open and welcome you in… They have made a little bed for you and got it all ready… The cover and the pillow are your favourite colour. They tell you that you can lie on it for a little sleep and they will look after you… You make yourself comfortable in the bed. It is soft and warm… The fairies are busy around you with their dusters… They love you and care for you… Enjoy being looked after. Close your eyes and fall asleep… Now it is time to leave the fairies… get up slowly, and leave the tree house… You close the door and climb back down the little ladder, till your feet touch the path… The fairies will always be there if you need them. Let's follow the path back down the little hill, etc.

(Use the rest of the **End Section** to complete this visualization.)

Into the Garden of Dreams

Pathway 23: The golden fish

Use the basic journey visualization (Pathway 20) to get as far as the big tree. This time do not stop to look at it, but use the following to continue on:

Let's follow the path up the little hill and past the big old oak tree… Today let's keep on the path which twists and turns and brings us down to a bubbling stream… The clear crystal water runs over the stones and just keeps going on and on. Stand on the bank and watch the clear water as it goes by…

As you watch, something swims past, in the water. Then it swims back up stream again. It is a golden fish… Kneel down on the bank and take a closer look… It flicks its golden fins and tail and swims over to us… It stops, and moves its head from side to side as it looks at you… Then all of a sudden it pops its head right out of the water… It says your name and says how special you are… It tells you what you are good at… and what it likes best about you… It has heard so much about you that it is very glad to meet you at last… You talk with the fish and find out its name… Then, it asks you if it can be your friend. You tell it that you will come back soon to see it. It is time now to leave the golden fish and the stream…

Follow the path up past the old tree… past the grass, etc.

(Use the rest of the **End Section** to complete this visualization.)

Into the Garden of Dreams

Pathway 24: The waterfall

Use the basic journey visualization (Pathway 20) to get as far as the big tree. This time do not stop to look at it, but use the following to continue on:

Let's follow the path up the little hill and past the big old oak tree… Keep on the path as it twists and turns and brings you down to the stream… Today you find that someone has put a flat pink stone right in the middle of the stream… It is meant as a stepping stone so that you can cross the stream. You take a little jump and land on the pink stone… Watch the stream water as it passes by the stone… and then jump over to the other side.

Now that you are on the other side, you are going to walk beside the stream until you come to some big rocks. You squeeze through a little gap between the rocks and find a waterfall. The crystal water tumbles down from a high rock… and splashes into a pool down below… The water is so clear and fresh that you go under its shower… When you are enjoying being under the water, the sun shines down and turns the water into dazzling rainbow colours. The water splashing down on you turns to your favourite colour… enjoy being showered… see and feel that colour… play and splash in the bright water… You can swim around in the shallow little pool of dazzling water… The sun goes behind a cloud for a minute, and the water becomes crystal clear again… You jump out on to the grass on the bank and dance in the warmth until you are dry… It is time for you to find your way back to the pink stone. Use it to jump over to the other side of the stream…

Follow the orange path up and past the tree… etc.

(Use the **End Section** to complete this visualization.)

Into the Garden of Dreams

Pathway 25: Meeting Owl

Use the basic journey visualization (Pathway 20) to take the children to the big old tree. Use the following to continue:

Today when looking up into the branches of the tree, you see a pair of big kind eyes looking down at you… They belong to Owl who says she has seen you in the garden before… She says your name and asks if you want to come up to visit the tree house… You go round to the little ladder at the back of the tree, just as she tells you… Carefully you climb the ladder, one step at a time, holding on at the sides… When you get to the top of the ladder you open the door and go into the tree house. Owl is waiting for you, perched on the back of a soft little armchair. It is a little wooden house with spaces for windows where you can look out into the branches of the tree…

A bird has built a nest on one of the branches… and a squirrel is scampering right to the top of the tree… Owl asks you to sit in the chair so she can chat to you…. You talk to her for a little while… she wants to know how you are getting on… Then she says she has a present just for you… It's just to show how special a person you are… She uses her beak to drop it into your lap… and you say thank you… It's time to go now so you put the present into your pocket or carry it carefully… You say goodbye to Owl… She tells you to come back anytime to talk to her. She lives in the garden…. Close the tree house door and start to come back down the ladder… one step at a time till your feet touch the orange path… Let's follow the path back down the little hill…

etc.

(Use the rest of the **End Section** to complete this visualization.)

Afterwards, in a Sharing ring (Pathway 10), the children can perhaps talk with the teacher about their own present from Owl.

Into the Garden of Dreams

Pathway 26: Owl's quest

Use the basic journey visualization (Pathway 20) to take the children to the big old tree. Use the following to continue:

Today when you get to the tree Owl is waiting on one of the lower branches of the tree… She thinks that you are ready now for her challenge. There is something important that she wants you to do… Somewhere in the world, she says, there is a tree that is you… You are to search the world until you find it… Then you are to come back and tell her what it is like… She gives you a piece of paper with some questions to answer about it… To help you look over the world, she says Eagle is waiting to take you high into the air… At that very moment Eagle swoops down… You climb on to its back… And when you are holding tight… it spreads its wings and soars into the sky… Up high over the garden it goes… and you look down at the world, the world of mountains… forests… rivers… deserts… cities and towns… ice… islands… Remember you are looking for the tree that is you… You will know it when you see it… have a good look… When you spot it way down there… point it out to Eagle… who will come down, down, gently to land beside the tree… Stand looking at the tree… Take out the piece of paper with Owl's questions on it… Remember these are about you, the tree…

What do you look like? Are you tall… small… straight… twisted… rough… What colour?… Do you have lots of branches and leaves, or just a few?

Where are you growing? In a garden… a park… on a mountain… in a street… in the desert… in a forest?

What is around you? Are there other trees… are you alone… is there a fence or wall round you… are there birds and animals?

What do you do for others in the world? What do you give to people… animals… or birds?

Who takes care of you? Is it a gardener… a friend or a caring person… how do you survive?

Once you've thought about the questions and found some answers, it is time to go back to the garden… Climb back on to Eagle… and fly along till you are back over the garden, and come down to land on a rock. Thank Eagle for the flight and make your way out of the garden following the path all the way to the gate… I'll open the gate so that we can all pass by… After we all come out, I close the gate… I am now going to count slowly. When I have said three, slowly open your eyes and look up at the ceiling… 1, ,. 3… Once your eyes are open… have a big stretch… and sit up straight again.

Into the Garden of Dreams

Pathway 27: Drawing

The Garden of Dreams

After using some of the visualizations, have the children draw their garden of dreams.

Use coloured felt tips to draw in all the things they remember from the visualizations.

The children might like to put in one thing they would like to see in the garden.

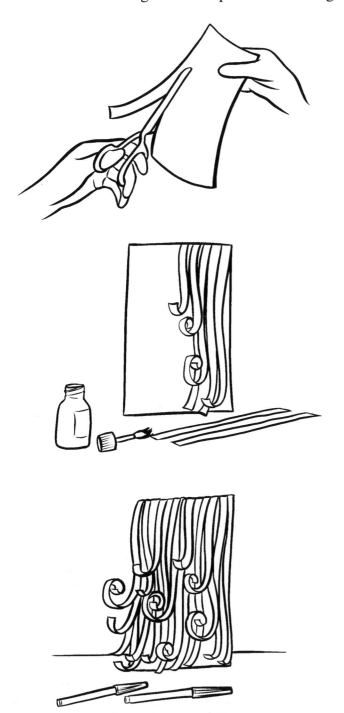

The waterfall

Draw the waterfall of coloured water, with the artist playing in it.

A magical waterfall paper sculpture can be made using an A4 sheet of paper and various textures of paper, all in toning shade of any one colour.

Wide and thin, long and short, strips and pieces are torn or cut from the shiny and textured paper. These strips are curled, folded or cut with zig zags or slashes, and then attached with glue at one end of the top of the backing sheet, portrait way round. The other ends remain free and all these various strips give the tumbling down effect of a waterfall.

A rainbow effect could be achieved using paper strips cut from a range of paper colours, or from rainbow coloured paper.

Into the Garden of Dreams

Pathway 28: Painting and craft

Trees in the garden

Ask the children to paint a tree. They can paint on separate sheets of paper, or arrange it so that four children can paint on the one large sheet at the same time.

You can precede the painting activity with a short visualization. This could take them to a garden where, after looking round, they look at one particular tree which they are drawn to. Teacher's questions during the visualization can focus the children's attention on the various parts of the tree. (See **Owl's quest** Pathway 26).

On another day, have the children quietly look at the tree they have painted. Tell them they are the tree, the tree is them. They are to write four sentences beginning with 'I am the… tree', and continue in the first person. Give them a specific amount of time for this task.

Make an impromptu garden with a large piece of green fabric, or several pieces of green paper. Scrunch up newspaper underneath to form little hills. The class or group sit round this garden in a sharing ring. They take turns to position their tree in the garden and then read out their sentences about themselves as the tree, to the others.

Into the Garden of Dreams

Pathway 29: Map making

The teacher or the children prepare quite large scale, coloured drawings and labels for some of the garden's most important features. These are laid out randomly on the table in advance of the actual map making.

Represent no more than six features for the first attempt at map drawing, e.g. the red gate, the orange path, the yellow sunflowers, the green tree, the blue stream, and the pink stepping stone. Rather than drawing them, the path and the stream can be shown using narrow, wavy-cut strips of orange or blue paper overlapped end to end. An actual piece of rose quartz could become the stepping stone. Scrunched up newspaper under the green cloth can be the little hill on which the tree stands.

Set the context for the task by explaining to the children, that the gardener is expecting some visitors from abroad, on the very day that he goes away on holiday himself. He feels that they will need some help to find their way around and has asked if the children could make maps for the visitors.

The model of the garden is built up as a kind of three dimensional map, before any drawing takes place. The children sit in a circle round a large piece of green fabric (approximately 1.5m by 2.5m) on which the drawings and paper are carefully positioned. As different children are adding each of the pre-prepared drawings and labels the teacher emphasizes the correct order. 'What is the next thing the visitors will come to?' A 'way in' arrow sign could be positioned near the gate.

Once the simple model map is complete, the teacher can role model how it can be represented with symbols, using a black pen and a large sheet of paper. The addition of a title and well-positioned labels are essential if the visitors are to understand the squiggles on the paper. The maps can be collected and sent to the gardener.

Pathway 30: Dream flags

Tell the children about prayer flags that are used in Tibet and Japan. Strips of paper or cloth are hung on trees to blow in the wind, to attract kind spirits and good fortune. Show them photographs, if possible.

They are going to write their own flags using the planning sheet first. Decide on colours for the different kinds of flags, if more than one flag is to be written, for example, yellow for dream, green for hope. Colour those words over with that colour on the planning sheet (SR/G). Give the children a certain amount of time to complete the planning sheet by themselves, in a quiet place.

On a different day they can write their hopes, dreams etc on coloured diamond shaped pieces of paper. These diamonds can then be folded in the middle, over a length of wool and glue put between the two halves.

The finished strand of six coloured triangle flags, like bunting, can be hung on a tree outside, or on a branch in a vase, or on a model tree they have made out of wire. A place for these model trees could be found in the school garden, and the flags left to flutter in the wind.

It is more effective if they are put outside. All the hopes and dreams etc float out on the wind to the universe.

Alternatively, each child could attach just one flag to a tree outside.

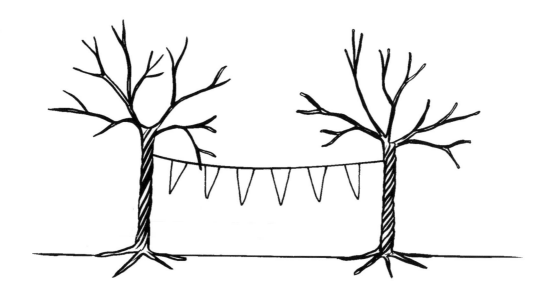

Into the Garden of Dreams

Pathway 31: Modelling trees

Trees can be modelled using eight strands of wire each about 20 cm long and bound with another strand of the same length. Five to six centimetres of the length at the bottom can be used to form the roots. These can be fixed to a thick card base using small rectangles of Mod-roc™ moistened with water. At the other end of the bundle, open out the strands of wire to form the branches. The branches and the trunk section in the middle can be bound round with layers of similar sized pieces of Mod-roc™.

When the Mod-roc™ is dry and hardened, the tree and base can be painted and decorated. The little tree could be modelled on the features of the tree from the *Owl's quest*. Alternatively, it could be a magical tree with sequins and jewels.

Into the Garden of Dreams

This activity is best done when the children have had lots of practice in visualization. Have Owl's questions written up large on the board or wall, and remind the children of them.

1:	What do you look like?		4:	What do you do for others?
2:	Where are you growing?		5:	Who takes care of you?
3:	What is around you?			

Keeping these questions and the answers in mind, the children are to draw the tree that is them in the octagon frame (SR/H). They then complete the sentences below, to answer the questions. You may wish to have them use the planning sheet (SR/I) after the drawing, in which case their good copy could be written on to the sheet (SR/J). Enlarge the sheet for less able children who find writing a challenge, or the teacher may scribe a word on each leaf in answer to the questions.

Into the Garden of Dreams

The trees below could be added to an on-going model of the garden, made initially to help with the map making. In positioning their trees, the children will need to decide where they want their tree to grow in the Garden of Dreams.

I am the green apple tree I stand in a colourful garden. The tree has lovely bright red apples on it and it has a house hidden behind the green puffy leaves. Look at the black ladders climbing up the green apple tree.

_____

I am long and smooth, with long tangly roots. I have blue spots on my smooth trunk and I have very long green and blue branches that hang down. I grow red hearts and a huge boa lives on me.

_____

I am a brown and green tree. I have lots of roots as well and I am bent over. I have got berries on me and a rock underneath me. There is a river at the back of me and there is a waterfall beside me.

_____

I am the dull tree and I am dirty and a bit peckish. My branches are quite long. On my branches are kinds of bushy leaves. Beside my tree is a gate that is quite old and broken.

_____

I am the 'fire tree' and I live in the centre of the garden. I have red and yellow colour as I get angry easily. There are no trees very close because I don't like to be crowded. My 'friends' are nice. They nicknamed me 'fire tree' but I don't mind.

_____

I am the crooked, bashed, autumn tree with its branches without leaves. I am the jagged tree with its twigs as sharp as thorns. I am the gnarled tree with its bark peeling off. I am the tree without green leaves. I am the tree with its roots everywhere. I am the lifeless autumn tree.

You are a star.
_____ years
old today.

You are a star.
_____ years
old today.

You are a star.
_____ years
old today.

You are a star.
_____ years
old today.

You are a star.
_____ years
old today.

You are a star.
_____ years
old today.

My name is

_____

_____

I am

_____

years old

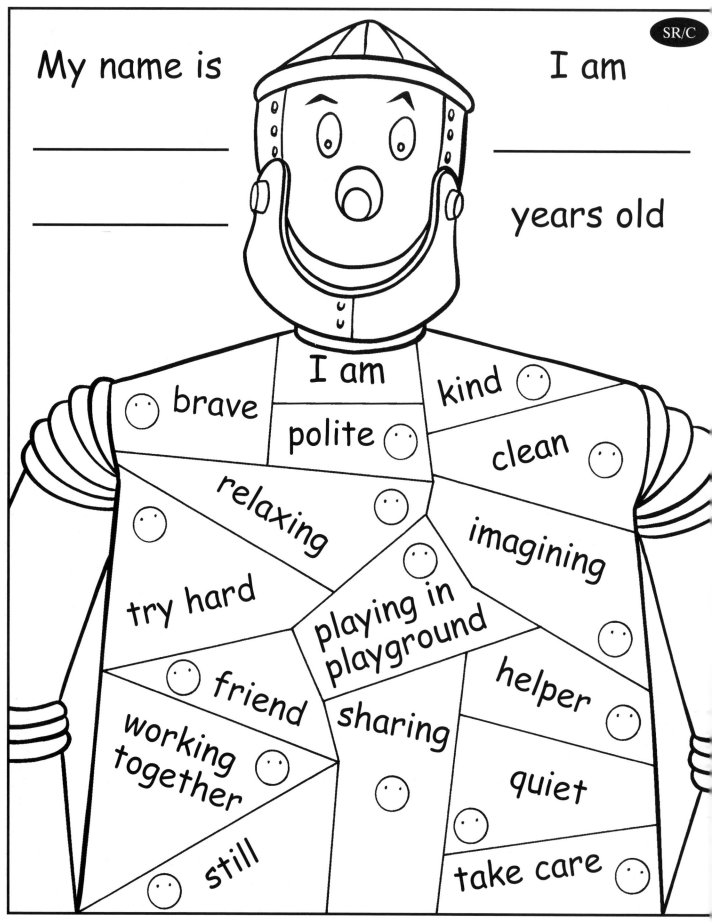

I am

brave

kind

polite

clean

relaxing

imagining

try hard

playing in playground

helper

friend

sharing

working together

quiet

still

take care

my symbols key: ✓ I am good at things

 I like   I am okay   ☹ I don't enjoy

My name is

I am

_____

_____

years old

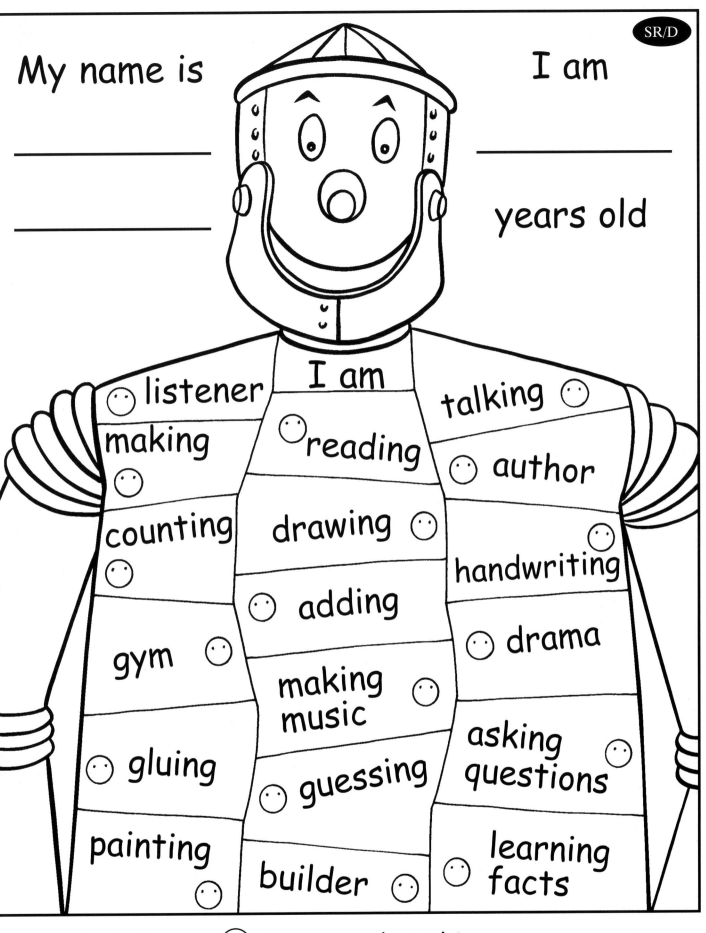

I am

listener

talking

making

reading

author

counting

drawing

handwriting

adding

gym

drama

making music

gluing

guessing

asking questions

painting

builder

learning facts

my symbols key: ✓ I am good at things

 I like   I am okay   I don't enjoy

Our class rules

	yes	no
	yes	no

be kind

be quiet

be tidy

walk

Dear Parents

Your child is starting an activity called Surprise Box with their class at school. Over the next few weeks each child will get a turn to bring the Surprise Box home.

When your child brings this box home, help them to choose an interesting household object (no valuables please) to place in the box and take into school. The rest of class will have the job of guessing what the object is, by asking your child questions about it.

The object chosen should be different to those objects already brought to school by the other children. Talk to your child about this.

Help your child to answer any possible questions that they may be asked in school.

Through this worthwhile activity we hope to develop your child's ability and skills in

• questioning and answering

• memory

• confidence

• self-esteem.

Thank you for your help.

Tree flags planning sheet

NAME:	
WORRY:	
FEAR:	
DREAM:	
HOPE:	
MESSAGE:	

Tree flags planning sheet

NAME:	
WORRY:	
FEAR:	
DREAM:	
HOPE:	
MESSAGE:	

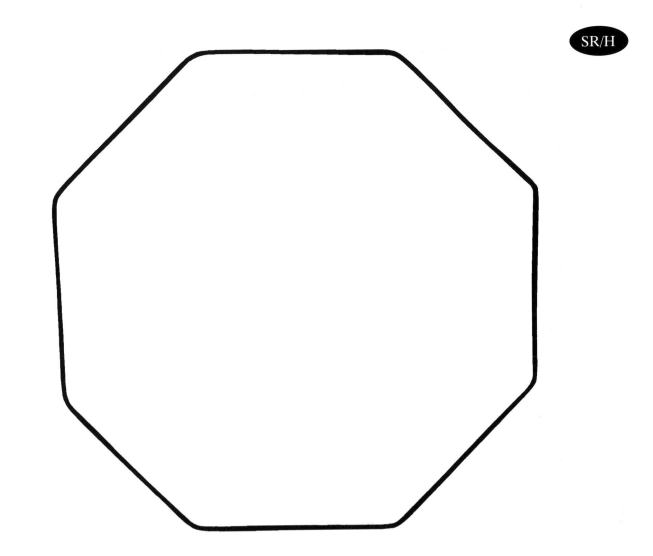

 I am

 I grow

 There are   around me.

 I give

                              takes care of me.

Planning sheet

 I am

 I grow

 There are

 I give

 takes care of

me.

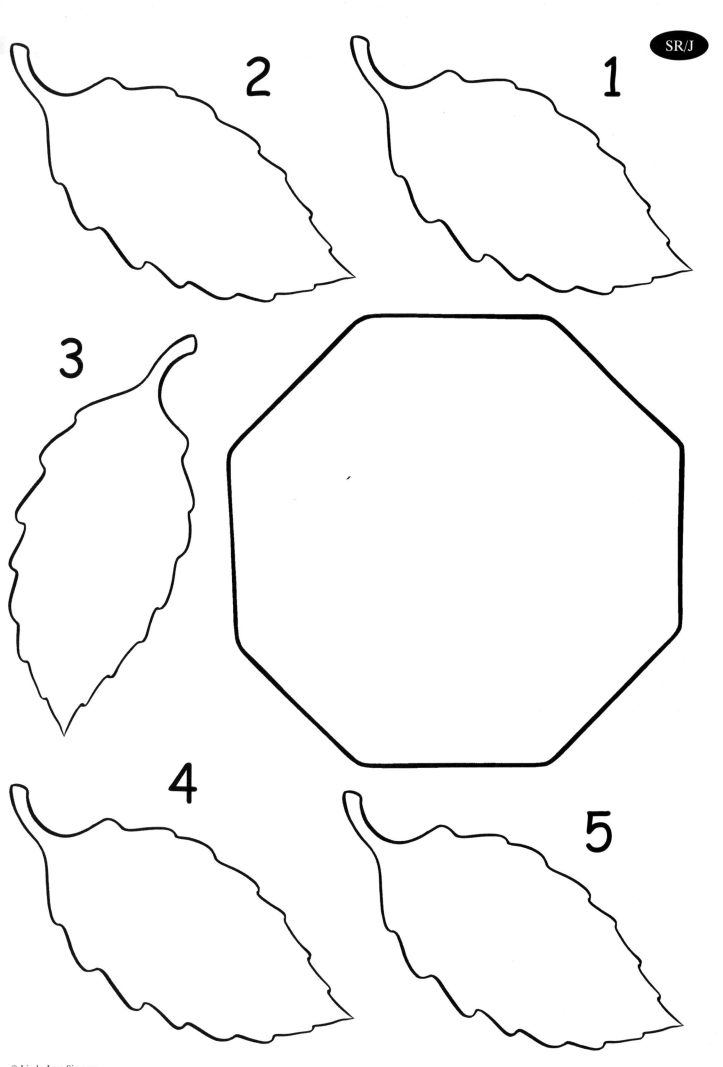